The Hard Stuff

CONTRACTS, TAXES, LICENSING, INSURANCE & LEGAL REPRESENTATION

Modern Artist's Handbook Vol 2

Gail Daley

COPYRIGHT

The Hard Stuff

6

The Hard Stuff

.

The Hard Stuff

THE HARD STUFF: TAXES, LICENSING & RECORDKEEPING

Most information for this section was taken from the following web sites: California State Board of Equalization (BOE) and IRS.gov. For more information or answers to specific questions, please go to those web sites. There is a lot of information to cover, so let's jump right in.

ORDINARILY SUBJECT TO SALES TAX

In general, retail sales of tangible personal property in California and other states are subject to sales tax. Examples of tangible personal property include such items as furniture, giftware, toys, antiques, clothing, and so forth.

In addition, some service and labor costs are taxable if they result in the creation of tangible personal property. For example, if you make a ring for a specific customer, you are creating tangible personal property. Therefore, the total amount you charge for the ring (including the charge for labor) would be taxable. This would also be the case if the customer provided the materials for making the ring.

However, labor costs for making repairs (resetting a diamond, for example) are not taxable since they do not result in the creation of tangible personal property. You are only repairing or reconditioning existing property.

Likewise, a labor charge to install or apply property that has been sold is not ordinarily subject to sales tax (*note*: the labor charge should be stated separately on the bill).

There are many rules governing what is taxable. Artists living in California are encouraged to call the BOE's Information Center **800-400-7115** or contact your nearest BOE office for information on what is taxable for your business. If you live in another state, I strongly urge you to check out your state's rules in this matter.

SALES TAX

Since I live in California, out of Necessity, I am somewhat familiar with California's rules concerning Sales Taxes. **WHAT IS TAXABLE?** Retail sales of tangible personal property in California are generally subject to <u>sales tax</u>. Examples of tangible personal property include such items as art, furniture, giftware, toys, antiques, clothing, and so forth. In addition, some service and labor costs are subject to sales tax if they result in the creation of tangible personal property. (Art commission?)

In some instances, retailers must pay use tax, rather than sales tax, to the BOE. The most common example of a purchase subject to the use tax is a purchase of an item for use in California from an out-of-state retailer. Out-of-state retailers who are engaged in business in this state are required to collect the use tax, whenever applicable, from the consumer at the time of making the sale.

The tax rate for sales and use taxes is the same.

Some sales and purchases are exempt from sales and use tax. Examples of exempt sales include, but not limited to, sales of certain food products for human consumption, sales to the U.S. Government, and sales of prescription medicine. For more information on exempt sales, California Artists please refer to California publication 61, *Sales and Use Taxes: Exemptions and Exclusions.*

WHO IS RESPONSIBLE FOR PAYING SALES TAX TO THE BOARD OF EQUALIZATION? As a seller, you owe the sales tax and are responsible for paying the correct amount to the BOE. If you do not pay the correct amount, you are subject to additional tax charges plus applicable penalties and interest charges.

INTERNET SALES

If you have a web site, you may want to increase your cash flow by selling your original art, prints or other items on the Internet. Most web site developers have a

PayPal option that will allow you to set up internet payments. The most common question about Internet Sales is are on-line sellers required to collect sales tax? That is not easy to answer because there is no consistent law regarding collecting sales tax on internet sales from state to state, and at present there is a hot debate on whether or not you can be required to pay sales tax to a state where you have no physical presence. It is probably safe to say however, that you should check out the rules set up for this in your particular state. To do this I can recommend this site: http://www.nolo.com/legal-encyclopedia/50-state-guide-internet-sales-tax-laws.htm

For Artists living in California, even if you sell 100% of your art online from home in a twelve-month period on auction or any other type of internet sites, you are still required to hold a valid California seller's permit. Even if you only sell three or more items considered tangible property, you could still be required to have the seller's permit. Internet sales are treated just like sales you make at retail stores or other outlets, through sales representatives, over the telephone, or by mail order. Artists located principally in California should read: Publication 109 - Internet Sales.

RE-SALE NUMBERS: WHO NEEDS ONE?

You must obtain a **seller's permit** (re-sale number) if you:

- Are engaged in business in California and Intend to sell or lease tangible personal property that would ordinarily be subject to sales tax if sold at retail.
- The requirement to obtain a seller's permit applies to individuals as well as corporations, partnerships, and limited liability companies. Both wholesalers and retailers must apply for a permit.
- If you do not hold a seller's permit and will make sales during temporary periods, such as Christmas tree sales and rummage sales, you must apply for a temporary seller's permit. Such permits are normally issued to selling operations lasting no longer than 30 days at one location.
-

WHAT DOES *engaged in business* mean? You are engaged in business in California if you:

- Have an office, sales room, warehouse, or other place of business in this state (even if the location is only temporary).
- Have a sales representative, agent, or canvasser operating in this state.

- Receive rental payments from the lease of tangible personal property in this state.

There are other activities that may qualify a selling operation as being engaged in business in California. Due to the various rules that apply, you should contact the BOE's Information Center **800-400-7115** or contact your nearest BOE office to determine if you must obtain a permit.

APPLYING FOR A SELLERS PERMIT

You can visit or call a nearby BOE office to obtain an application. Or, you can arrange to have an application mailed or faxed to you by calling **800-400-7115**. Applications can also be downloaded from Forms and Publications Section of the BOE website.

(*Note*: You will need to mail or bring in the completed application since we must have your original signature. You should make a copy for your records.)

IF I APPLY FOR A PERMIT, WHAT INFORMATION IS NEEDED TO COMPLETE AN APPLICATION?

You will be asked to furnish:

- Your social security number (corporate officers excluded).
- A photocopy of your driver license to ensure the accuracy of the information provided and to protect against fraudulent use of your identification numbers.
- The name and location of a bank where you have an account.
- Names of suppliers.
- Name of person maintaining your account.
- Names and address of a personal reference.
- Anticipated average monthly sales and the amount of those sales that are not taxable.

Additional information may be required.

If you have a business partner, or if the business is managed by corporate officers or limited liability company managers, members or officers, those persons will also be asked to furnish some of the information listed above.

IS INFORMATION REGARDING MY ACCOUNT SUBJECT TO DISCLOSURE?

Yes. While most of the information you provide to the BOE is confidential, some is subject to public disclosure, such as the information on your seller's permit and the closeout date of your business, if applicable. Under certain conditions, your account information, including underreporting and outstanding liabilities, may be shared with the other government agencies.

FILING REQUIREMENTS

WHAT IS A SALES AND USE TAX RETURN? A sales and use tax return is used by seller's permit holders to report the payment of sales and use taxes to the BOE. Permit holders are required to file a tax return. Electronic Filing (e-filing) is the BOE's prescribed method for filing sales and use tax returns.

WHEN DO I FILE THE TAX RETURN? When you obtain your seller's permit, you will be instructed to file your tax return on a monthly, quarterly, or annual reporting basis.

Your tax return is due after the close of each reporting period. In other words, if your period closes on June 30, your tax return and payment is due on July 31, the last day of the following month. If the due date falls on a Saturday, Sunday or legal holiday, returns are due the following business day. Check the Calendar of Due Dates for your filing basis.

You must file your tax return and pay by the tax due date whether you efile, mail, or hand-deliver the return. Failure to receive a return or reminder from us does not excuse you from the requirement to file.

DISCLAIMER: THE INFORMATION IN THIS BOOKLET IS FOR GENERAL INFORMATION PURPOSES ONLY; IT IS NOT INTENDED TO BE TAX OR LEGAL ADVICE. EACH SITUATION IS SPECIFIC; CONSULT YOUR CPA OR ATTORNEY TO DISCUSS YOUR SPECIFIC REQUIREMENTS OR QUESTIONS.

BUSINESS LICENSES

IS A SELLER'S PERMIT THE SAME AS A BUSINESS LICENSE?
No. You should contact your city and/or county business license department to obtain a separate business license. To locate the department, check the government pages of your telephone directory (for example, look for the terms license or business license under City Government Offices and County Government Offices).

EIN NUMBERS: An Employer Identification Number (EIN) is also known as a Federal Tax Identification Number, and is used to identify a business entity. Generally, businesses need an EIN. You may apply for an EIN in various ways, and now you may apply online. This is a free service offered by the Internal Revenue Service. Do you need an EIN? The IRS has a list of questions at the following link http://www.irs.gov/businesses/small/article/0,,id=97872,00.html. .answering yes to one of them will automatically send you to the on-line application processes.

DISCLAIMER: THE INFORMATION IN THIS BOOKLET IS FOR GENERAL INFORMATION PURPOSES ONLY; IT IS NOT INTENDED TO BE TAX OR LEGAL ADVICE. EACH SITUATION IS SPECIFIC; CONSULT YOUR CPA OR ATTORNEY TO DISCUSS YOUR SPECIFIC REQUIREMENTS OR QUESTIONS.

FEDERAL & STATE TAXES

Artists and writers generally fall under the designation of "self-employed" for Federal and State tax filing purposes. This means you will probably need a Schedule C and form SE added to your tax return. As a self-employed individual, generally you are required to file an annual return and pay estimated tax quarterly.

With few exceptions, Self-employed individuals must pay self-employment tax (SE tax) as well as income tax. SE tax is a Social Security and Medicare tax primarily for individuals who work for themselves. It is similar to the Social Security and Medicare taxes withheld from the pay of most wage earners. In general, anytime the wording "self-employment tax" is used it only refers to Social Security and Medicare taxes and not any other tax (like income tax).

Before you can determine if you are subject to self-employment tax and income tax, you must figure your net profit or net loss from your business. You do this by subtracting your business expenses from your business income. If your expenses are less than your income, the difference is net profit and becomes part of your income on page 1 of Form 1040. If your expenses are more than your income, the difference is a net loss. You usually can deduct your loss from gross income on page 1 of Form 1040. But in some situations your loss is limited. **See** Pub. 334, Tax Guide for Small Business (For Individuals Who Use Schedule C or C-EZ) for more information.

You have to file an income tax return if your net earnings from self-employment were $400 or more. If your net earnings from self-employment were less than $400, you still have to file an income tax return if you meet any other filing requirement listed in the Form 1040 instructions.

COMMON AUDIT ISSUES FOR ARTISTS & GALLERIES

Information for this blog was taken from
REG   121584-05   page   523
*http://www.irs.gov/businesses/small/artic
le/0,,id=254019,00.html* - 77.3KB

Probably the one agency that terrifies
Americans the most is not the NSA, but the
IRS and being audited by the IRS ranks up
there with being on some mobster's hit
list. The best way to avoid being audited
is to know what items will be considered
red flags by the IRS. The following are a
few audit issues looked at by the IRS that
may be found in the examination of an art
gallery or home studio.

- Unreported income through cashed
  checks from galleries to the artists
  leading to related returns to be
  examined.
- Barter transactions between artists
  and others in the art field.
- Taxability and inventory assessment
  issues for trades between gallery
  owners and artists.
- Avoidance of state sales taxes.
- Treatment of ordinary income as
  capital gains by mischaracterizing
  inventory as investments.

- Identification of sources who failed to file/report transactions through "cost of goods sold" by studying cancelled checks and payment/transaction records.
- Framing costs not properly recorded.
- A History of losses or very high travel and entertainment costs with low gross receipts suggesting potential Activity Not Engaged in for Profit pursuant to I.R.C. § 183.
- Sales of artwork disguised as "loans" secured by art as collateral and possible "money laundering".
- Other "financial status" indicators which show an artist's or gallery owner's reported income is incompatible to his or her lifestyle.
- Potential issue on Non-Resident Alien Artist, Art Galleries, Dealers and Brokers (International Referral Required).
- Artwork being deducted as a charitable contribution at fair market value rather than adjusted cost basis and/or not being taken out of cost of sales.
- Business use of the home.

If the gallery purchases its inventory, there should be a very detailed inventory listing showing the purchase date, the purchase price, any restoration and framing costs, the sales date, and price.

If the gallery sells on consignment, there will be a system in place to track consigned items. This system will generally contain the artist's name, his or her address, a description of artwork, the date on which the artwork was received by the gallery, the asking price by the artist, and any other specific terms. It also indicates the date the piece was sold, the sales price, and terms of the sale.

The sales invoice for an art piece needs to display the buyer's name, address, date of sale, amount paid (if not fully paid), terms of any installment plan, sales tax, shipping charges, and framing charges if it is the type of artwork that would require framing.

Since artists are not offering a service, galleries are not required to complete a Form 1099 for the payments made. However, artists should receive a consignment check either <u>monthly</u>, at the time of sale, or at a time specified in an agreement between the artist and the gallery.

The best way to keep issues like those above from impacting your career as an artist is to keep good records for your home studio/gallery. If you sell your art, it is considered income and over a certain amount, it must be reported as such to the IRS on your federal taxes. If you participate in a booth event, you are usually required to have a seller's permit, collect sales tax, and then report and pay that sales tax to the State. Art is a business as well as a creative endeavor. Losing your art can be a financial loss. Not being aware of losing money because you don't keep track of costs can create a huge problem.

Hey, relax; this isn't as difficult as it sounds! Let's take this one step at a time, using one piece of work. Step one: decide in what form you are going to keep your work log. While it is very helpful to have this information stored on a computer, artists were tracking their work using paper files long before computers became popular. I personally prefer using a computer worksheet, however, all of this stuff can be put on a sheet of paper and kept in a binder. For the initial record,

I recommend a single sheet or worksheet per art piece. (Please see the Art Information Sheet in the Sample section)

- ITEM 1—a pictorial image of your work. This can be in the form a printed photograph, a slide or a digital image. If your work is 3-deminsional, be sure to take photos of all sides of the work. Since this image is not going to be used to reproduce the work, a small, low-resolution image will suffice. The image should be large enough to see details of the work, clear and without blurring.
- ITEM 2—the title of your work, size, style/genre and when it was finished.
- ITEM 3—a brief description of the work (use complete sentences—why will become clear later). Optional—I also like to keep a kind of diary as to what I wanted to achieve, why I chose this image, and what was going on in my life when I created this art piece.
- ITEM 4—Keywords to be used when downloading the photo of your art to your web site or other internet media.
- ITEM 5—Show and exhibit record is a list of what shows or exhibits were entered, when they took place and if the art won awards.
- ITEM 6—wholesale and Retail price. This is probably the hardest thing for an artist to decide on—how much to charge for an artwork! What is the difference

between Wholesale and Retail? Wholesale is always lower than Retail. Your wholesale price at a minimum should cover the cost of what it cost you to create the art, plus any gallery commission fees and hopefully with a small profit margin. Retail price for an art piece should cover all this plus what you as an artist feel the art is worth. I realize this is very subjective but most of art *is* subjective.

- ITEM 7—Incidental information such as the date you formally copyrighted the work, cost of the copyright, etc. More about copyrights later in the Copyright section.
- ITEM 8—If you had limited editions of a painting or photograph or copies of a sculpture made, when, how many , how much it cost to make them, how many sold and how much you made when you did.
- ITEM 9—the date you sold the original art and the name and address of the Buyer.

SPECIAL TYPES OF TAX DONATIONS

ART DONATIONS:

Many artists often get hit up to donate art to charities. There is nothing wrong with this and it can get you some publicity within your community. A word of warning about deducting art on your tax return: the IRS usually won't allow you to deduct the selling price of the donated art, only the cost of materials and labor. Sorry, but that is the way it reads.

DEDUCTION OF BUSINESS MILES

Deduction of miles driven for business is a legitimate expense. The IRS defines Business Miles as including distances traveled using your vehicle while working on behalf of your employer or miles driven between jobs. For example, if your employer required you to drive from your office to visit clients using your car, that mileage would be deductible. The IRS does not allow you to claim a deduction for miles that you drive from your home to your job. This is considered "Commuting" by the IRS and is not deductible. For example, traveling to a client's home or business to paint or draw them might be considered Commuting; check with your accountant.

QUESTIONS: If I work out of my home as an independent contractor, can I claim mileage to work sites and back home? Can I deduct trips made to the bank and post office? What if I make business-related trips from my home office and stop to do personal errands? How do I figure the mileage?

ANSWER: Yes, your mileage to work sites and back are business miles that must be supported by written documentation of where you went and how many business miles you traveled. Trips to the bank and post office also qualify as business mileage if documented. Trips for personal errands are ignored. The end result of your records should be business miles for the year (with a backup written log) and total miles driven for the year. To document your total miles driven, take your odometer reading at the beginning and end of the year. The IRS often looks at the odometer reading on auto repair bills to see if your total miles are reasonable. You will need to check with the IRS for their current mileage rate.

Most office supply stores sell mileage booklets for you to keep in your car. But you can write the information in a simple notebook and then use the sample spreadsheet sheet and the end of this book on your computer.

QUESTION: I drove about 8,000 miles last year for my home business. I have some receipts, but I didn't log all the miles. Is an estimate OK? Can I still take the deduction if I don't have all the supporting information?

ANSWER: No, estimated business miles are not allowed to support your tax deduction. The tax court disallowed the auto expenses in 2009 for the owner of a real estate brokerage firm and her employee in <u>Engle v. Commissioner</u>. The taxpayer admitted that their reported mileage amounts were estimates. In a summary opinion they held that due to lack of substantiation the taxpayers were not entitled to the auto deduction. I personally know of someone who lost their house when they claimed "estimated" mileage on their taxes! It isn't worth it!

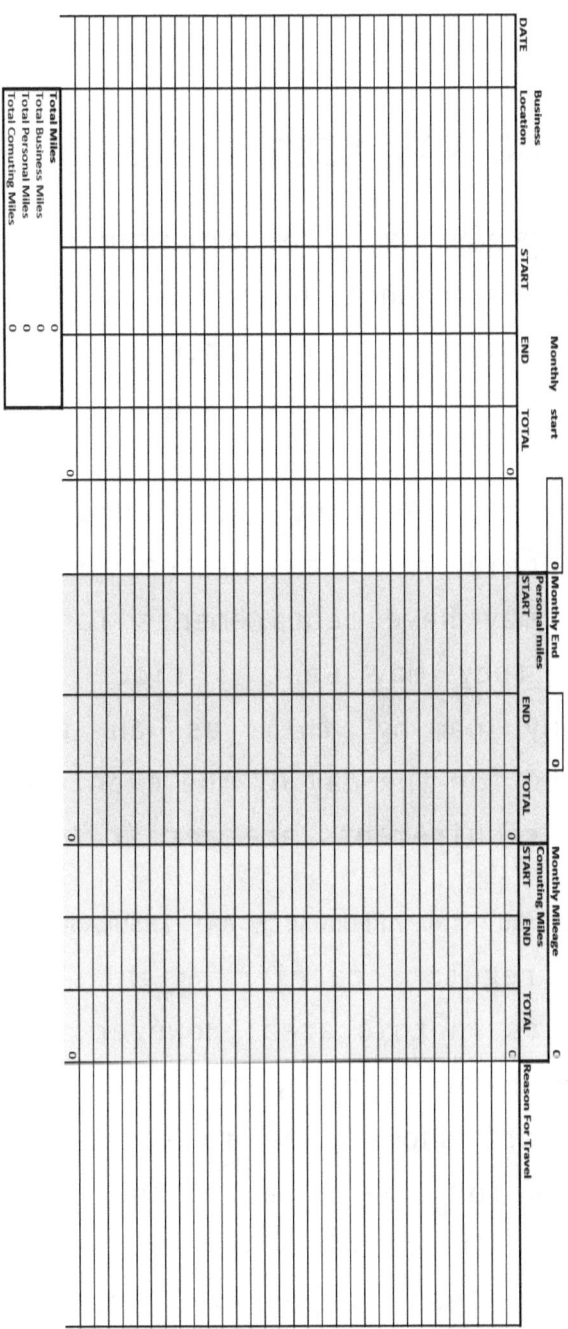

DO YOU NEED INSURANCE?

INSURANCE REQUIREMENTS FOR BOOTH EVENTS: insurance questions cannot be answered by anyone other than your insurance carrier. At a minimum, you probably want some sort of theft and personal liability coverage but I don't have any knowledge of what California requires or recommends. The venue may have requirements for coverage also; they may want a rider from your company naming them as an additional insured for the day of the event. Whatever their requirements are—*get it in writing!*

HOW DO YOU FIND AFFORDABLE ART INSURANCE COVERAGE? Your regular carrier might not have contacts in this area; However, Local art groups have to carry event insurance for their art shows. Get in touch with them and ask for a referral to their insurance carrier. The carrier they are using may be a lot less expensive than someone unfamiliar with this type of coverage.

QUESTIONS TO ASK THE CARRIER: what protection do I as a vendor need for my art or books and my possessions? Possessions refers to your laptop, etc. What protection do I need if someone is hurt within my stall? What protection does the venue carry for fire, theft, personal liability? What about fire or other damage caused by an accident in another person's booth that then adversely affects mine? Ask all the "what if" questions you can think of and then make your own determination about participating. Also, check into whether there is an insurance contract and what the terms of the contract may be before signing and have your insurance agent look it over first as well as an attorney if there are things you don't understand. Never assume, always ask for clarifications and *get them in writing*.

If you are displaying your art somewhere like a restaurant, other space or gallery, most likely you will need to arrange with the owner regarding theft or damage to your art. My carrier won't cover my art outside my home unless I want to pay big bucks, which I can't afford. Many art shows carry riders to this effect also.

DO I NEED ADDITIONAL COVERAGE IF I AM WORKING OUT OF MY HOME? The answer to that is, maybe. Unless your homeowners insurance has an exclusion forbidding you to work out of your home, you probably are covered for fire and theft since the art you create can be considered personal property. If you need to make a claim, the carrier will require documentation. That is why it is important to keep good records of what you painted. You should consult your insurance carrier as to how much they will cover for each art piece. *Don't make assumptions and get stuff in writing.*

DO YOU NEED A CONTRACTOR'S LICENSE?

Most states regulate construction contractors. In California, the Contractors State License Board (CSLB) was created to protect consumers by licensing and regulating California's construction industry. Visual Artists and visual art do not usually come under construction laws, however there is one facet of the visual art world that does come under this law: Murals. Wikipedia defines murals as any piece of artwork painted or applied directly on a wall ceiling or other large permanent surface. For instance if you are invited to paint a mural on the wall of your doctor's office and you were paid more than $500, under California construction laws, you might need a Contractor's License. Artists may not be aware that they could be violating California state licensing laws if they painted or otherwise created a mural on a permanent structure i.e. a house or office wall, outside building, etc... The C-33

Painting and Decorating license section covers painting a mural on a permanent structure. Individuals who limit their practice to that of an artist could also be covered under either D-64 (non-specialized contractor designation) or C-61 (Limited Specialty contractor classification). If an artist is paid more than $500 (labor and materials) to paint a mural on a permanent structure, they are subject to state contractor licensing laws under the Business and Professions Code Section 7026. As of this year, California still has no license classification for specifically for an artist painting art on walls or buildings, so artists are forced to apply for the general painting contractor's license. FYI Other states may have different requirements.

Requirements for C-33 licensing can be pretty stiff (and expensive); you must pass the state law and business exam in addition to the trade exam related to painting. Cost: Initial application fee is $300, the application to add a supplemental Classification $75, Home improvement salesperson (HIS) registration fee $75, etc... Then it has to be renewed each year. In addition to the license itself, CSLB always requires worker's comp insurance on most projects if anyone but you does any part of the work.. Then there are the bond requirements for a General License; "D" class licenses on the other hand may be less expensive to obtain since potential contactors are only required to pass the law and business exams. However, the tests themselves are quite complicated and most potential contractors actually take courses designed to help them pass the tests (this is not free either).

DO YOU NEED A LAWYER?

It seems never to occur to most artists (with some notable exceptions) to have a lawyer look over the contract their new Gallery or licensing company wants them to sign. Why not? Well, a couple of reasons might be that the artist is just so thrilled to have an actual walk-in gallery or licensing firm offering to display or sell their work that the artist overlooks making sure their rights are protected, or more probably, the artist simply can't afford to hire an attorney.

There are several types of legal contracts an artist might be involved with listed below.

- A contract commissioning a piece of art.
- A consignment contract with a gallery to sell your work,
- A licensing agreement to sell prints, cards or commission work to be translated into other art forms (plates, tiles, textiles, etc.).
- An agreement with an agent to sell or advertise your work.
- An agreement with a venue (non-gallery) to display or sell your art.
- Booth rental space at an event.

When are the times when you should have someone with legal experience take a look at what you are signing? Well, if you can afford it, anytime you want to be paid for your work, but if you are a starving artist, probably you won't be able to afford a lawyer's $60/hour retainer (this is cheap by the way). However, you *do* have some other options. If you ever find yourself in need of legal representation, you can try Lawyers for the Arts. Most states have either a volunteer lawyers for the arts organization or regular lawyers for the arts who, if you ask for it, will sometimes give you a pro bono consultation to see want you need. Even if you don't see the need to have legal advice on every little thing, there are some issues you need to make sure are covered in any contract you enter into.

- If this is a commission sale, when is to be completed and how soon afterwards are you paid?
- Is the Gallery or Agent requiring exclusive rights?
- When are payments due from consignment sales?
- How long does the consignment last?
- If there is a reception who pays for it?
- Who hangs the art?

- If hanging your art causes damage who pays for the repairs?
- FYI If the gallery or venue goes out of business make sure your art cannot be considered part of the gallery assets or they could be sold to pay business debts in which case you won't receive any payment for your work.

BUSINESS EXPENSES

Art is a business, and like any business, it is needful to keep track of expenses as well as income. In the Document & Spreadsheet section is a suggested list of income and expenses. This is only a suggested list. You may find that you need different or more or less items to track, depending on the kind of art you do.

I can't say this often enough; back up your data! Keep back-up copies of these items in a separate place. Up-date your back-ups monthly. Once your records are lost due to computer crashes, natural disaster or any other reason they are gone.

You should keep three types of records:

- A photo log with both high- and low-resolution photos of your work, kept separately from your desktop computer. A working copy can be kept on the desktop, but be sure and back up your files each month onto a separate disc or jump drive.

- A program that tracks income and expenses.
- A record of each piece of art created and its disposition or current location.

I would recommend QuickBooks to track your expenses and income. You can simply use a spreadsheet program to track expenses but it is very time consuming. QuickBooks, while a little on the expensive side is easy to use and easily transitions into tax software programs such as Turbo Tax when it comes time to file your income tax. Below is a list of suggested expenses.

SUGGESTED DEDUCTIBLE EXPENSES

ASSETS

       Personal account
       petty cash
       Accounts Receivable
       Employee Advances
       Inventory Asset
       Undeposited Funds
       Accounts Payable
       Sales Tax Payable
       Opening Bal Equity
       Retained Earnings

INCOME

       Keepsake Boxes
       boutique receipts
       Fee Income
       Instruction/School

Book Sales

       NON-FICTION SALES
       Paperback
       Royalty Payments
       E-books
       NOVEL SALES
       Paperback
       E-books
       Royalty Payments

Product Sales

       pamphlets
       cards
       prints
       magnets
       posters

OTHER REGULAR INCOME

       Other Income

        Original Art

       Art Commissions

       Show awards

       Digital Art Sales

       Reimbursed Expenses

INTERNET

       Web site Sales

       Internet Sales (other than web site)

EXPENSES

Advertising

ART SUPPLIES

       Canvas

       Digital Art Prints & Framing

       :framing

       Painting

       Paints

AUTOMOBILE EXPENSE

       Fuel

       Maintence

       Registration

       Repairs

BOOK SALES

       copyright fees

       Cover Design

       Editing services

NOVELS

       Advertising

       Bar code purchase

       Buy books 4 local distribution

       Copyright fees

       distribution costs

printing costs

sales commissions

NON-FICTION

Advertising

Bar code purchase

Buy books 4 local distribution

Copyright fees

distribution costs

printing costs

sales commissions

GALLERY EXPENSES

Gallery fees

booth Fees

Gallery commission fee

Show entry fees

GENERAL EXPENSES

charity:10% tithe

Cost of Goods Sold

Depreciation Expense

Dues and Subscriptions

Equipment Rental

Insurance

Liability Insurance

Interest Expense

Finance Charge

Loan Interest

Mortgage

Licenses and Permits

Meals and Entertainment

Miscellaneous

Rent

Repairs

Building Repairs

OFFICE EXPENSES

Cell Phone

computer Hardware

paper

Postage

Printing and Reproduction

Printing costs -

Computer Repairs

SOFTWARE UPGRADES & SUBSCRIPTIONS

storage boxes

Telephone

Toner

Web Site development &e-bay fees

Pay Pal fees

Printing Costs

Shipping costs

OUTSIDE SERVICES

PROFESSIONAL FEES

Accounting

Legal Fees

Editing

Tax Preparation

REPAIRS

Equipment Repairs

Janitorial

TAXES

Federal

Local

Property

Sales Taxes paid

State

TRAVEL

Food

Misc Expenses

Motel

UTILITIES
        Gas and Electric
        Water
OTHER EXPENSES

CHOOSING A SOFTWARE PROGRAM

Art is a business, and like any business, it is necessary to keep track of expenses as well as income. While you can do this by hand, nothing beats a computer program to track stuff! I have been searching for a comprehensive program for my art business for years. While there are some all-inclusive programs beginning to be developed, I have usually found some flaw in the program; either they were hard to use, or had an incompatible photo program for thumbnails of my art, etc. There _are_ a couple of new companies with programs designed for artists out on the internet.

**DISCLAIMER**: Please keep in mind that as I have no practical experience with any of these programs except Working Artist, it is up to you to check them out for yourself and decide if they will fit your needs. Here are some links to potential art software sites along with what information I have on them:

Art Looks Software:

http://www.artlooksoftware.com/Downloads/ Introduction.pdf **(Free evaluation copy available**) Current pricing is £150.00 (I assume this is British pounds or some type of Euro symbol). Any time a site offers you a free evaluation, it is worth checking out.

GY*ST http://www.gyst-ink.com/ This program Retails for either $59.00 or $129.00 depending on whether you want just the basic system or their Pro program.

Art Systems:

http://www.artsystems.com/products/system .htm this system says it will link to QuickBooks, web manager and has a system for I-Pad. It is also VERY expensive; licensing for this puppy runs anywhere from $5,000 down to $795.00.

Working Artist:

http://workingartist.com/

Retails out for between $139 -- $154 with upgrades for $59. This one comes in 4 separate editions 1) a studio edition designed for agents representing several artists, 2) The artist edition, designed the single artist to manager their business. The site also claims to have an edition for Art Fairs and for Galleries, but I wasn't able to access them by clicking on them. This is the only one of these software programs I have any actual working knowledge of, and it was about 10 years ago that I tried to use a free trial download. At that time, I experienced considerable difficulty in uploading photos of my work into the program, as it would not accept jpeg versions for some reason. I assume they would have corrected this issue in the intervening time.

Masterpiece Manager:

http://www.masterpiecemanager.com/artistf nb.html this one says it will manage inventory, contact, point of sale, has art web site templates, e-mail marketing and is available for MAC & PC. This is not that unusual as ALL of the software programs say they have both MAC & PC versions. Pricing for individual artists is $29/month, which works out to about $348 a year. Like Working Artist, this set up also has different programs for Galleries, stores consignment stores, museums, etc.

If you don't want to purchase an expensive program, you can simply use a spreadsheet to track income and expenses but this method it is very time consuming, although I do have one available that is already set up. For myself, I currently use QuickBooks to track expenses and income. QuickBooks, while a little on the expensive side is pretty user friendly and easily transitions into tax software programs such as Turbo Tax when it comes time to file your income tax. Unfortunately, I have heard rumors that it doesn't mesh as well with Apple products as it does PCs. If you simply want to go the spreadsheet route and manually track stuff, you can access copies of my

spreadsheet   system   at
http://www.thepracticalartist.com.

Yes, Virginia, I am actually using three programs to track my art and my expenses. QuickBooks for income and expenses, two spreadsheets that tell me where my art is at any given time; (Current Location Report and Painting Information Sheets) to track awards, income from each painting or prints made from it. I also use a photo file with different sized images of my art for various uses (webpage, large-sized prints, and specific sizes for on-line show entries).

For Photo Editing I use Photoshop Elements because it is less pricey than the full Adobe editing program and as a painter, I really don't need the maximum amount of bells and whistles you get with the full Adobe Suite. However if you are using a Mac instead of a computer, pay the subscription for the full suite. Photoshop not only works differently on a Mac, but the App instructions will be different.

I can't say this often enough; back up your data!

SAMPLE DOCUMENTS

Downloadable copies of these can be found at www.thepracticalartist.com

ARTIST-GALLERY CONSIGNMENT AGREEMENT

ARTIST: (Name, Address, and Telephone number):

_____

_____

_____

_____

And

THE GALLERY: (Name, Address, and Telephone number):

_____

_____

_____

_____

Hereby enter into the following Agreement:

1. The **Artist** appoints **The Gallery** as agent for the works of art **("the Artworks")** consigned under this **Agreement,** for the purposes of exhibition and sale. **The Gallery** shall not permit the Artworks to be used for any other purposes without the written consent of the Artist. This agreement applies only to works consigned under this **Agreement** and does not make **The Gallery** a general agent for any other works.

2. Exclusive Representation. The **Artist** does **not** appoint **The Gallery** as their sole representation throughout "Specific area" to sell or otherwise make available for acquisition to the public, the **Artist's Artworks.** However, the **Artist** does appoint **The Gallery** as their sole representative of the artworks listed below on the inventory list to sell or otherwise make available for acquisition to the public.

3. Consignment. The **Artist** hereby consigns to **The Gallery,** and **The Gallery** accepts on consignment, those **Artworks** listed on the attached **Inventory Sheet** which is a part of this **Agreement.** Additional Inventory Sheets may be incorporated into this **Agreement** at such time as both parties agree to the consignment of other works of art. All **Inventory Sheets** shall be signed by **Artist** and **Gallery.**

4. Authority of Accepted Artist's Works. Works of art may be accepted for consignment only by any person designated by either of them in writing as authorized to accept works of art hereunder. **The Gallery** may reject artworks at the Owners discretion.

5. Warranty. The **Artist** hereby warrants that he/she created and possesses unencumbered title to the **Artworks,** and that their descriptions are true and accurate.

6. Duration of Consignment. The **Artist** and **The Gallery** agree that the initial term of consignment for the **Artworks** is to be 12 months, and that the **Artist** does not intend to request their return before the end of this term. Thereafter, consignment shall continue until the **Artist** requests the return of any or all of the **Artworks** or **The Gallery** requests that the Artist take back any or all of the **Artworks** with which request the other party shall comply within 30 days.

7. Transportation Responsibilities. Packing and shipping charges, insurance costs, other handling expenses, and risk of loss or damage incurred in the delivery of **Artworks** from the **Artist** to **The Gallery** are the responsibility of the **Artist.** Packing and shipping charges, insurance costs, other handling expenses, and risk of loss or damage incurred in the delivery of **Artworks** from **The Gallery** to the **Artist,** shall be the responsibility of **The Gallery.**

8. Responsibility for Loss or Damage, Insurance Coverage. The Gallery shall be responsible for the safekeeping of all consigned **Artworks** while they are in its custody. **The Gallery** shall be strictly liable to the **Artist** for their loss or damage (except for damage resulting from flaws inherent in the **Artworks**); to the full amount the **Artist** would have received from **The Gallery** if the **Artworks** had been sold. **The Gallery** shall provide the **Artist** with all relevant information about its insurance coverage for the **Artworks** if the **Artist** requests this information.

9. Fiduciary Responsibilities. Title to each of the **Artworks** remains in the **Artist** until the **Artist** has been paid the full amount owing him or her for the **Artworks;** title then passes directly to the purchaser. All proceeds from the sale of the **Artworks** shall be held in trust for the **Artist. The Gallery** shall pay all amounts due the **Artist** before any proceeds of sales can be made available to creditors of **The Gallery.**

10. Notice of Consignment. The Gallery shall give notice, by means of a clear and conspicuous sign in full public view that certain works of art are being sold subject to a contract of consignment.

11. Removal from Gallery. The Gallery shall not lend out, remove from the premises, or sell on approval any of the **Artworks,** without first obtaining written permission from the **Artist.**

12. Pricing; Gallery's Commission; Terms of Payment. The Gallery shall sell the **Artworks** only at the Retail Price specified on the Inventory Sheet. The **Gallery** and the **Artist** agree that the **Gallery's** commission is to be_____% percent of the Retail Price of the **Artwork**. Any change in the Retail Price, or in **the Gallery's** commission, must be agreed to in advance by the **Artist** and **the Gallery**. Payment to the Artist shall be made by **the Gallery** on the 15th of every month, and will include all commissions due for any/all artworks sold. **The Gallery** assumes full risk for the failure to pay on the part of any purchaser to whom it has sold an **Artwork**. _____ (Artist initial) _____ (The Gallery initial)

13. Framing. If **the Gallery** will be framing the **Artwork, The Gallery** and the **Artist** agree that **The Gallery's** expense will be factored into the retail price and full compensation for framing will be given to **The Gallery** upon the sale of **Artwork**. Should the **Artwork** be returned to the Artist as outlined in this agreement, the **Artist** and **The Gallery** are equally responsible for the wholesale cost of the framing expense.

14. Promotion. The Gallery shall use its best efforts to promote the sale of the **Artworks. The Gallery** agrees to provide adequate display of the **Artworks,** and to undertake other promotional activities on the **Artist's** behalf. **The Gallery** shall identify clearly all **Artworks** with the **Artist's** name, and the **Artist's** name shall be included on the bill of sale of each of the **Artworks. The Gallery** and the Artist shall agree in advance on the division of artistic control and of financial responsibility for expenses incurred in **The Gallery's** exhibitions and other promotional activities undertaken on the **Artist's** behalf.

Promotion type:
Cost:
Gallery to Pay %
Artist to Pay %
Promotion Date:

15. Reproduction. The **Artist** reserves all rights to the reproduction of the **Artworks** except as noted in writing to the contrary. **The Gallery** will not permit any of the **Artworks** to be copied, photographed or reproduced without the written

59

permission of the **Artist.** In every instance of such use, the **Artist** shall be acknowledged as the creator and copyright owner of the **Artwork. The Gallery** shall include on each bill of sale of any **Artwork** the following legend: "All rights to reproduction of the work(s) of art identified herein are retained by the **Artist:** _____."

16. Accounting. A statement of accounts for all sales of the **Artworks** shall be furnished by **The Gallery** to the **Artist** on the 15th of each month, with the payment of all commissions due. The **Artist** shall have the right to inventory his or her **Artworks** in the gallery and to inspect any books and records pertaining to sales of the **Artworks.**

17. Termination of Agreement. Notwithstanding any other provision of this **Agreement,** this **Agreement** may be terminated at any time by either **the Gallery** or the **Artist,** by giving a sixty (60) day written notification of termination from either party to the other. In the event of the **Artist's** death, the estate of the **Artist** shall have the right to terminate the **Agreement.** Within thirty days of the notification of termination, all accounts shall be settled and all unsold **Artworks** shall be returned by **The Gallery.**

18.   Procedures   for   Modification. Amendments to this **Agreement** must be signed by both **Artist** and **Gallery** and attached to this **Agreement.** Both parties must initial any deletions made on this form and any additional provisions written onto it.

19.   Miscellaneous. This **Agreement** represents the entire agreement between the **Artist** and **The Gallery.** If any part of this **Agreement** is held to be illegal, void, or unenforceable for any reason, such holding shall not affect the validity and enforceability of any other part. A waiver of any breach of any of the provisions of this **Agreement** shall not be construed as a continuing waiver of other breaches of the same provision or other provisions hereof. This **Agreement** shall not be assigned, nor shall it inure to the benefit of the successors of **The Gallery,** whether by operation of law or otherwise, without the prior written consent of the **Artist.** In any proceeding to enforce any part of this contract, the aggrieved party shall be entitled to reasonable attorney's fees in addition to any available remedy.

This **Agreement** shall be governed by the law of the State of California.

Artist:_____Date:_____

Gallery: _____ Date:_____

Contract to begin on: _____

and end on: _____

ART CONSIGNMENT LIST
- TITLE OF ART:
- MEDIUM:
- SIZE/DIMENSIONS:
- RETAIL PRICE
- GALLERY COMMISSION:

(Make one of these for EVERY piece of art you have in EVERY gallery.)

AGREEMENT TO HANG ART IN A VENUE
(I.e. Restaurant, office, bank, etc.)

This is an agreement between the Artist: _____

Address: _____, _____, _____

hereafter known as "Artist" to hang artworks in the Venue whose address is below.

And The business establishment: _____

Address: _____, _____, _____

hereafter known as Venue to hang or display art in the Venue.

Agreement to begin on: _____

and end on: _____

- The artist will bring art to the Venue on the designated dates to be mutually agreed upon with the Venue. An inventory list of Art will be provided to the Venue.

- **HANGING ART:** Art will be hung by the artist either using a hanging system supplied by the Venue, or by the artist putting up screws or nails to secure the art. If the artist puts up screws or nails, the artist agrees to do everything possible to minimize the damage to the Venue's walls by making as few holes as possible (in other words the artist will make every effort to utilize screws or nails already in use when changing out the art).

- Art must be hung within twenty-four (24) hours of being received at the Venue Location.

- The artist will supply an identifying tag alongside each piece of art identifying the artist, medium and price of the art.

- Although the Venue may veto individual pieces of art as not suitable for their establishment, the artist will choose which art pieces to bring in. The artist usually finds that a variety of art (abstracts, landscapes, still Lifes, figures, animals, etc) is visually agreeable.

- The art will be changed at regular intervals, mutually agreed upon by the artist and the Venue. The usual period is three (3) months.

- **SELLING THE ART**: The Venue may choose to handle sales of the art for the artist, taking a twenty percent (20%) commission on the art, or allow sales to be handled by the individual artist. If the sale is handled by the artist, any employee of the Venue who facilitates a sale is eligible to receive a 3% commission from the artist. Sales should be recorded on the Art inventory list. **Please initial below which option is chosen by the Venue.**

- _____ (initial) The Venue chooses to handle sales of the art and take a 20% commission from each sale. Payment to the artist is to be given within two (2) weeks of the final sale.

- _____ (initial) The Venue chooses to allow all sales of art to be handled directly by each artist. The artist agrees to pay the facilitating employee the three percent (3%) commission within two (2) weeks of the final sale.

- **REMOVAL OF ART**: Once hung, the art will remain in place except during regular change outs of the art by the artist unless sold. Unless the art is being sold to a customer, the Venue may not remove the art or take it down from the display area without three (3) days advance warning to the artist. The art may not be taken off the premises other than by the artist or the artist's agent.

- **OWNERSHIP OF THE ART**: All art hung remains the property of the artist and is not to be considered an asset of the Venue in cases of closure or financial reverses. If the Venue closes for other than normal business hours, notice must be given within (3) days of closure so that the artist may remove the art.

_____ (initial) the artist will hang art on: _____

The art display will be changed by the artist every three months.

Artist: _____Date: _____

Venue: _____Date: _____

ART CONSIGNMENT LIST
- **TITLE OF ART:**
- **MEDIUM:**
- **SIZE/DIMENSIONS:**
- **RETAIL PRICE**
- **VENUE COMMISSION:**

AGREEMENT FOR COMMISSION OF ARTWORK

The Artist _____agrees to paint/create artwork as described below

_____

_____

_____

Size/Dimensions _____

Medium: _____

For the Client named: _____

for the sum of $_____.

A non -refundable deposit of 25% of the painting price is due upon The Artist beginning the painting. The Artist will start the painting on: _____, The Painting will be completed by: _____,

The remainder of $_____ is due upon delivery of the painting to

_____

The Client agrees to take Delivery of the painting within 30 days of the start of the painting and the Artist agrees to complete it within that time period. Framing will be done by _____

The Artist retains copyright of all paintings or commission work. No prints,

Internet distribution or video presentation of artwork may be done without the express written permission of The Artist.

NON-DESTRUCTION: The Purchaser will not permit any intentional destruction, damage or modification of the Painting.

NOTICE: A notice, in the form below must be permanently affixed to the Painting, warning that copyright, ownership, etc., are subject to this contract.

TRANSFEREES BOUND: If anyone becomes the owner of the Painting with notice of this contract, that person shall be bound to all its terms as if he had signed a sales agreement when he acquired the Painting.

EXPIRATION: This contract binds the parties, their heirs, and all their successors in interest, and all the Purchaser's obligations are attached to the Painting and go with ownership of the painting, all for the life of the Artist and the Artists' surviving spouse plus 21 years.

ATTORNEYS' FEES: In any proceeding to enforce any part of this contract, the aggrieved party shall be entitled to reasonable attorney's fees in addition to any available remedy.

If the finished artwork is not acceptable to the buyer, or final payment is not received within 15 days of delivery, the artwork will be returned to The Artist.

The Artist may then sell or otherwise dispose of it as the artist sees fit.

If the Client does not or cannot pick up the art when it is finished and after final payment has been made, There is a $_____ delivery fee for shipping.

Delivery to be made to the following address: _____

_____ The Artist

Date _____

_____ Client

Date _____

ART INFORMATION SHEET

The Art Information Sheet is a record of each piece of art you have created. Over our lifetimes as an artist, all of us will probably create hundreds of pieces of art. It may seem anal and a waste of time when you first start out to take the time to make a record of each individual art piece you create. Just wait -- when you are trying to remember which landscape of Monterey, or which of 30 red abstracts or which painting of magnolias out of the 15 you painted in the past 20 years that you entered into a show, or whom you sold it to, you will come to see the value of good records. If you keep the information sheet up to date, you will always have a documentation of your work, and where it has been, who bought it, if you successfully sold prints or additional castings from it etc.

You will also have a handy record of everything you might need to post it on your web site, enter it into a show, write a press release or create a blog for it

- Record No:
- QR code or Url
- Art Title
- Size
- Media
- Physical Description
- Keywords
- Finish Date
- Copyright Date
- Primary Color
- Secondary Color
- Style/Genre
- Wholesale Price
- Retail Price
- Date Sold:
- Buyer's Name and Address:
- Notes
- Narrative:
- Thumbnail of Art (Below)

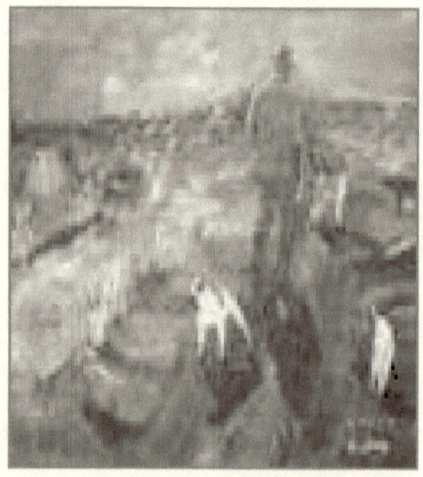

ART LOCATION SHEET

Unlike the Art Information Sheet which was designed to track single pieces of art, this sheet is a quick overview of where all of your art is being shown or exhibited and is designed to work in tandem with the Art Information Sheets.

The Art Location Sheet is a record of where each piece of art you have created is being shown or exhibited and what shows or exhibits you have entered it into in the past. Over our lifetimes as an artist, all of us will probably create hundreds of pieces of art. It may seem anal and a waste of time when you first start out to take the time to track this type of information. Just wait -- when you are trying to remember which land- scape of Monterey, or which of 30 red abstracts or which painting of magnolias out of the 15 you painted in the past 20 years that you entered into a show, or whom you sold it to, you will come to see the value of good records. If you keep the location sheet up to date, you will always have a documentation of where it has been.

By keeping track of this kind of information, you won't lose art you spend hours creating because you can't remember where it is, or find yourself in the embarrassing position of having to ask someone else if you are currently displaying your art in their show or exhibit. You especially won't find yourself making excuses to a show coordinator or director of exhibits as to why you are entering the same piece you entered last year into their show or exhibit!

The simplest way to keep this record is on a spreadsheet. Use the titles on one line of the spread sheet:

- Record No.
- Title:
- Medium
- Subject
- Current Location (Name of show or Venue)
- Installation or Receiving Date:
- Pick Up Date

The columns after pick up date only need the heading: Past Shows and year entered. Sample booklets found on

www.thepracticalartist.com

FOR WRITERS/AUTHORS

This contract is very similar to the one used by Artists. It is to be used when an author agrees to allow a bookstore, or other venue to display copies of their books for sale.

AUTHOR CONSIGNMENT AGREEMENT WITH BOOKSTORE OR VENUE

The Author _____agrees to leave the item(s) (See list below) on consignment with the Venue _____for the period beginning: _____ and ending on _____. The items will be covered under The Venue insurance policy for theft or damage for the time agreed on above. The Agreement may be extended on a month-to-month basis upon mutual agreement of both parties or ended upon 30 days written notice by either party.

For publicity purposes, the Author agrees to provide a biography as well as a brief info statement about the subject of the book or item.

The Venue agrees to accept the books, Posters or other items connected to the books for sale on a consignment basis In the event of a sale, The Venue will collect a commission of 20% (twenty percent) of the retail price. A Month-To-Date sales report will be available to the Author on request and will be sent to The Author along with a check for the author's percentage of sales at the end of each month.

It is understood that the author will accept no less than the listed wholesale price for the following item(s).

- Book Title
- Description (Hardback/Paperback)
- Author
- Wholesale Price
- Retail Price
- Venue Commission (20% of the difference between the wholesale price and the listed retail price)
- No of Copies supplied

Author _____

on_____   .

The Seller Venue accepts the items(s) on consignment and agrees to pay author for copies sold on a monthly basis or if none are sold that month to furnish a MTD sales report to the author.

Unsold books will be returned to Author in original condition. The Author is responsible for delivery and pick up of the items.

Author's Contact Information:

Phone # _____

E-Mail: _____

Make payments to:

Author or Publisher Name

_____

Author/Publisher Mailing Address

_____

Please indicate your acceptance by signing in the space provided for your signature.

Venue & Date _____

Author & Date _____

GAIL'S OTHER BOOKS

NON-FICTION

The Complete Modern Artist's Handbook

PAMPHLETS

Introduction To The Internet #1
The Hard Stuff - Handbook #2
Art Show Basics - Handbook #3
Framing on a Budget - Handbook #4
Are You Making Money? - Handbook #5

FICTION

SPACE COLONY JOURNALS

Options Of Survival
Destiny Rising
Tomorrows Legacy
The Interstellar Jewel Heist
The Designer People
Alien Trails
Quantum Light

PORTAL WORLD TALES

ST. ANTONI - THE FORBIDDEN COLONY

Warriors of St. Antoni
The Enforcers
The Gaslight Bandits
The Portal Lawman
Cradle of Fire
The Clone Initiative*

MAGI OF RULARI

Spell Of The Magi

Magi Storm
Magi Paladin*

*ETA and titles are subject to change

ABOUT THE AUTHOR

Gail Daley is a self-taught artist and writer with a background in business. An omnivorous reader, she was inspired by her son, also a writer, to finish some of the incomplete novels she had begun over the years. She is heavily involved in local art groups and fills her time reading, writing, painting in acrylics, and spending time with her husband of 40 plus years. Currently her family is owned by two cats, a mischievous young cat called Mab (after the fairy queen of air and darkness) and a mellow Gray Princess named Moonstone. In the past, the family shared their home with many dogs, cats and a Guinea Pig, all of whom have passed over the rainbow bridge. A recent major surgery on her stomach and a bout with breast cancer has slowed her down a little, but she continues to write and paint.

A NOTE FROM GAIL

Thank you for reading this book. Reviews are bread and butter to independents like me, so it would be much appreciated if you could write a review and share it on the site where this book was purchased.

If you would like to know when my next books are coming out, please follow me on social media sites or sign up to receive E-mail notices:

https://books2read.com/author/gail-daley/subscribe/1/72820/

E-mail lists are never shared with 3rd parties under any circumstances. You will only receive notices about upcoming books.